A Call to Reason
Losing our Manhood

Developing Positive Images in African American Boys

Dr. (MAJ)Khallid Shabazz

Those who profess to favor freedom and yet deprecate agitation, Are men who want crops without plowing up the ground.

They want rain without thunder and lightning.

They want the ocean without the awful roar of its waters.

This struggle may be a moral one; or it may be a physical one; but it must be a struggle.

Power concedes nothing without a demand.

It never did, and it never will.

Fredrick Douglas

August 4, 1857

-Excerpt from a speech on the West India Emancipation, delivered at Canandaigua (In Quarles 1969, p. 354)

The college drop-out rate for African-Americans, since the 1980s has risen 69 percent. Researchers began to explore reasons for this lack of achievement due to the negative outcomes associated with the underachievement of the African-American male (Lan, & Lanthier, R.2003). The purpose of this study is to examine the theoretical proposition from Bandura's (1986) Theory of Learning that environment and ethnicity and gender make a difference to the measures of locus of control, self efficacy, and self esteem. No prior studies have examined these relationships specific to the African-American male adult population in a highly structured environment. This study examines the veracity of a foundational principle of Bandura's Theory of Learning as applied to African-American males. This study will include multidisciplinary approaches seeking a way to educate our African American boys. The population will look at public schools, charter schools, military students along with the Afrocentric vs. non Afrocentric approach to education and its effects on this population.

DEDICATION

This dedication is with love to all the young African American men outside the system who want to be successful caretakers of their families, but feel alienated from the American dream. I was once angry at the system that incarcerated me mentally but learned how to channel my anger, not at the system or other men, but at myself; to be better, to be smarter and to be a stronger man for my wife, daughters and especially my son to show him what manhood could be.

I was once afraid and education allowed me to sustain myself in this difficult journey inside a system that seems to engulf African American males in its jaws without peril. To the African American mothers who pray, cajole, and whoop their children to inspire them because they know their boys are smart I commend you for your pain and your effort. My mom did all the above and I finally got it after many years. Thanks moms and the few fathers who stuck around even though life has been a living hell for you personally. You are the wind beneath my wings. I am dedicating my life and my death to sacrifice all that I am to intently pass on inspiration and to leave a legacy of learning for the future generations of African Americans to truly understand that it is possible to do the impossible. I also would like to dedicate this work to my grandparents, my father, mother, brother and two sisters. I love you very much. I hope I have made you proud although I didn't follow your chosen path for me. God willing, you respect me for being a thinking person and making a choice of my own. In addition, great thanks go to Jarvis Christian College who gave me an opportunity to go to school when other schools would not accept me because of my mediocre, subpar high school grades. I thank you for the environment that allowed me to believe in myself at a crucial time in my development.

Biography:

Dr. Khallid M. Shabazz (U.S. Army, Major)

Khallid Shabazz is a native of Alexandria, Louisiana. He holds a Bachelor of Science degree from Jarvis Christian College in Hawkins, Texas. He holds three Masters Degrees. They include a Masters in Ethics and Leadership, (Duquesne University) a Master's of Science in Islamic Studies (The Graduate School of Islamic and Social Sciences) and a Masters of Educational leadership (TUI University). Lastly, he also holds a Doctor of Philosophy in Educational Leadership, also from TUI University.

Dr. Shabazz's military education includes the Primary Leadership Development Course, Chaplain Basic and Advanced Officer Course. He entered the U.S. Army in 1991 as a cannon crewmember and quickly rose to the rank of sergeant. In October 1999, he was commissioned as a Captain. His previous military assignments include Baumholder, Germany; Fort Polk Louisiana; Bamberg, Germany; Fort Jackson, South Carolina and Guantanamo Bay, Cuba. He also deployed to combat with the 1-227 Aviation Brigade serving in Taji, Iraq as a Battalion chaplain and the theaters only Imam ministering to Muslims solders throughout the region. . Currently Major Shabazz is serving as a U.S Army Ethicist in Ft Sill Oklahoma.

Dr. Shabazz has a long list of awards including the Bronze Star, three Meritorious Service Medals, Joint Army Commendation, the Army Commendation and Achievement Medal, the Army Achievement Medal, two National Defense Service Medals, the Armed Forces Expeditionary Medal, the Global War on Terrorism Expeditionary Medal, the Iraqi Campaign Medal, the Army Service Ribbon, three Overseas Ribbons and the NATO Expeditionary Medal. He has been awarded the Humanitarian Award for Outstanding Volunteerism and was inducted into the Order of Saint Barbara, for service to the Field Artillery Corps. He is married to the former Rhonda Wright of Wills Point, Texas they have three children Yvonne 24, Jalen 18, Najala 13.

Copyright @2010 Khallid Shabazz All rights reserved

ISBN:978-0-557-57581-7

TABLE OF CONTENTS

FORWARD	7-10
PROLOGUE: What others are saying about the deficit in school system.	11
CHAPTER 1 **Why We Raise this Problem Endangered Species?**	13
Ethnicity, Self Esteem and Education	14
CHAPTER 2 **Life or Death**	18
Self-esteem, Self-efficacy and Locus of Control	19
CHAPTER 3 **Does a student's belief matter?**	23
Open Dialogue	26
CHAPTER 4 **Two Worlds Two Souls**	30
Environment and Ethnicity	31
Conceptual Framework	38
CHAPTER 5 **Which Theory is Most Effective?**	39
Afrocentric vs. Non Afrocentric Education	40
Societal Expectations	42
Teacher Expectation	43
CHAPTER 6 **Stereotype Threat**	45
CHAPTER 7 **Race and Prison**	48
Table 1	50
Conclusion Community Questions	51-52
Military pictures	56-58
References	59-64

Forward
By
Ibraheem Raheem

"Verily, God does not change the condition of a people until they first change the condition of themselves" Holy Qur'an 13:11

Know thyself...this is the key to all other knowledge and therefore success or failure in life. Though quoted in various ways, this statement is at the core of coming into full adulthood and the spark that leads a man to reaching his full potential. However, the preceding verse from the Qur'an is a reminder that the "condition of a people" closely resembles the people's sincere effort of self examination and inner desire to change. In this book Dr. Khallid Shabazz seeks to look at this issue of self examination and inner desire as it manifests in current forms and modern trends in education and the implications this has on the condition of African American males in America.

Since the first invasions of the Hyskos, Greek, Roman and Arab nations of the African continent, there has been a need to keep hidden the outstanding achievements of African people. Accordingly, the prevailing impression of African peoples throughout the world is that "history" as told in most educational systems introduces a derogatory image of Africans. All the while the same "history" sees fit to ignore the great contributions made by Africans in past and present times. Such an educational system is discouraging to say the least and leaves the African American student with very little desire or enthusiasm to thrive in this environment.

In his book *The African Origins of Civilization Myth or Reality* (1974) Dr. Chiekh Anta Diop through his research in anthropology, history and DNA brought to light the significant place Africans played in the history of human civilization. His relentless approach opened doors that were previously closed in terms of how Africans were viewed pertaining to their contributions to history in the areas of mathematics, science and medicine. He challenged the existing biases of these bodies of knowledge originating in Europe as well as proving that Africa was the location of the first humans through the use of radiocarbon research. It is on this premise that the African American community must leap forward and take pride in educating our youth about our own history as well as seeing ourselves as being able to achieve whatever we invest our minds and energy into.

As pointed out in this book there is no better time than the present to address the issues facing African American males. Because of the alarming rates of our African American male youth in prison, dropping out of school, stuck in poverty or laid to rest prematurely in the cemetery, now is the time to search for solutions that play a part in reversing the contributing factors that lead to the absence of the African American male in society. What is the African American male's place at home? Where is his place in today's work force? Where does he exist in relationship to the Black woman? How does he take back his dignity and respect in society and lead his family? The answers to these questions are shrouded in access to quality education as well as an education that teaches African American males to love themselves.

Dr. Bill Cosby is another leader that exemplifies the importance of self examination as key to reversing the current condition of our community. Though critical and hard to swallow, Dr. Cosby admonished the African American community in his "Pound Cake" speech for taking a passive approach to the core issues of morality, parenting, and education. Though his views were met with criticism and in some cases outrage, his main point; which I see related to the earlier quote from the Qur'an 13:11, was for the Black community to look within and stop blaming outside forces for things that are self inflicted and are within their reach to change about themselves.

From the foundation of a quality and esteem building education comes the dawn of a reversal of roles for the African American male. He can find his place as a leader as opposed to a follower, a producer as opposed to a destroyer, a giver as opposed to a receiver and an overall asset opposed to a liability. This book seeks to provide a road map to understand many of the contributing factors to our own condition and motivate us to take responsibility for our own success. Facing these challenges and overcoming them are at the root of the most critical efforts relating to the existence of a vibrant and competitive African American community.

However it is unavoidable when seeking to understand the challenges facing the African American community specifically the African American male without becoming aware of the issues of discrimination. Dr. Martin Luther King in his famous "I Have a Dream" speech stated;

> "But one hundred years later, we must face the tragic fact that the Negro is still not free. One hundred years later, the life of the Negro is still sadly crippled by the manacles of segregation and the chains of discrimination. One hundred years later, the Negro lives on a lonely island of poverty in the midst of a vast ocean of material prosperity. One hundred years later, the Negro is still languishing in the corners of American society and finds himself an exile in his own land. So we have come here today to dramatize an appalling condition".

In all due respect we must ask today how much of this reality of the African American's social condition still rests solely upon racism? Dr. King gave his life for the cause of Civil Rights but how have we made it count for anything? Claiming ignorance and turning a blind eye to what we can "do for self" is no longer acceptable.

Since the inauguration of the first African American President of the United States President Barack Obama, the myth that an African American was unable to achieve in this country was shattered. Amidst the discrimination, racism, and limitless doubters from within and from outside of the African American community President Barack Obama was able to achieve the highest office of leadership in the world mostly due to his access to the greatest education the world has to offer. The question becomes how do we show that this reality is at the forefront of our success and future as a community? I believe Dr. Shabazz deals with some of the answers to this question by calling us back to the importance of education in resurrecting the African American male.

Dr. Naim Akbar in a lecture "Brothers let us Heal Ourselves" issues the challenge;

> "We embrace the image and the behavior of dogs willing to be the sex symbol of the society because it is easier to relate with our smaller "head" rather than our big head. We prefer to be sperm donors and boast about the offspring we have produced rather than engaging in that scary and difficult job of being a father to a young boy or a young girl."

These soul piercing words get at the root of the identity African American males have bought into in today's society. Critical indeed but the above words are again rooted in principles laid out in the Qur'anic verse 13:11 and the idea of having a true knowledge of self and what real history states instead of a superficial and meaningless history pieced together that contributes to the poor self image and negative approach to life often portrayed in music, books and film about the Black male.

The choice is yours, and the future of our youth hangs in the balance of this choice. The time for excuses is over. This book can serve as a motivation to communities across the nation if taken seriously. Get involved in the issues facing the African American male by embracing the points raised in this book. It is time to look within and then make changes that will cause a reversal in our community before it is too late. This is not someone else's problem it is our problem. Therefore we must find our own solutions and execute them in our own ways. This book is a proposal to do just that.

PROLOGUE

What others are saying about the
African American deficit in the school system

Since manhood has been historically a complex task for Black males it is imperative that the right environment of positive role models should be used as socialization tools (Wyatt, S.T. (2000, p.24).

Jenkins (2006) identified specifics about the challenges of educating and socializing young Black males: "The underachievement, lack of inclusion, and backward progression of African American men within American society, and particularly within the educational arena, has once again surfaced as a trend that demands immediate attention" (p. 127).

Robinson and West (2001) explained that discrimination is a factor hindering Black males from advancing through the educational pipeline.

Hale (2001) mentions that by sending Blacks to inferior schools, the result is inferior skills, which helps White America maintain the oppression of Blacks. Hale believed that under the guise of freedom and opportunity, Blacks are blamed for their own plight. However, she also notes that racism is the culprit preventing Blacks from achieving educational parity with their White counterparts.

Dr. Julie Hare expressed that the role model without success is like a castrated stallion facing a herd of wild mares...inspired and excited, but without internal motivation sufficient to actualize, manifest or consummate the magnitude of the inspiration." (The Chicago Defender)

According to Lundy (2003), Blacks who subscribe to the mindset of "acting White," view academically inclined Blacks as abandoning their Black cultural identity and rejecting their own cultural norms. Blacks have formed an oppositional culture stemming from the oppression, enslavement and discrimination they have experienced in America. This oppositional culture acts as an obstacle between Black and White America, and also provokes Blacks to persuade their same-race peers to devalue academic success because of its association with "acting White."

Drs. Nathan and Julie Hare both maintain that the solution will not rest in improving teaching methods, as they currently feel "we have too many techniques." They see the battle being won increasingly outside the classroom, in what they call the "class-world."

Chapter 1

Endangered Species?

In this work, I will attempt to explain various myths and facts concerning the prevailing thought of the condition of African American males. African American males have become an endangered species, in that they have a 69 percent dropout rate from high school, they are disappearing from American colleges at a horrific rate, and are entering into America's prison system at a more rapid rate than any other ethnicity and or group in American history. The title, Losing our Manhood, is intentional in that with the current failure of our young African American boys our manhood is being usurped, taken over and pushed into the waste basket of unemployment, high prison rates, and boys masquerading as men leaving our young women manless, fatherless and husbandless.

This work will look into some ways of combating this decline by considering a change of environment as "An" avenue that should be explored as an option. I sought to pursue this direction because positive results in African American males have been produced by a number of programs that introduce same sex charter schools, military institutions and or schools that focus on specific afro-centric education. The research showed a change of environment produced significant improvement in self-esteem and self-efficacy of African American males. Why? *Because of, purpose, specified teaching and mentoring.*

In schools in Australia and elsewhere, a number of educators have argued that low self-esteem in minority students can be reversed if the culture shock of schooling is reduced. That is, most minority students develop low self-esteem as a result of culturally insensitive schooling.

These educators feel if more "culturally relevant teaching" was conducted, then the self-esteem of minority students would improve (Rubie & Townsend, 2004). This approach derives from studies in the U.S. of how increased "Black consciousness" would help improve African-American student's self-esteem (Okech & Harrington, 2003).

Ethnicity, Self Esteem and Education

Okech & Harrington, (2002) suggest that Western social scientists have a very myopic concept of what intelligence, self esteem, locus of control and self efficacy are. They argue that if a child's ethnic identity is fostered then the child would have better self-esteem thereby helping them to achieve in all areas of their life. This approach again derives from studies in the U.S. of how increased "Black consciousness" would help improve African-American student's self-esteem (Okech & Harrington, 2003). These approaches are based on a number of theoretical models of how one forms a healthy ethnic identity.

Cross developed a model in the 1960s which distinguished between four phases of the formation of ethnic identity. Cross's four stages are pre-encounter, encounter, immersion and internalization. In this construct, "each of these phases is described by an individual's perceptions, feelings and attitudes toward other African-Americans, Whites, and the self (Okech & Harrington, 2002).

For example, an African-American student existing in the pre-encounter stage acts according to a deeply held stereotypes and has little awareness that he or she is living according to an idea of his or her ethnicity as imposed upon them by others. During the encounter and immersion phase, one begins to become more aware of their ethnicity as distinct from others. They also pass through various phases of animosity and reconciliation with their own and other ethnic groups. According to Cross's model, an individual can also become stuck in various stages. Such may be the case of an African-American who becomes a promoter of Afrocentric ideology (in opposition to Whites), or even someone who militantly opposes White ideology without seeking resolution. Cross's final phase, internalization, involves developing a realistic sense of the locus of one's ethnic group in the world, in relation to other groups (Okech & Harrington, 2002).

The intent of Okech & Harrington's language is to urge consideration to the myriad of ways that people not only learn, but also how they assess different situations to protect their locus of control and self esteem. The purpose of this book is to explore different theories of learning to assist in the fortification of the African American male. These young men are not only failing at an alarming rate, but are made to feel ashamed of their strengths because they have been characterized in stereotypes by the larger society. It is incumbent that African American professionals intercede and support our African American children (and their innate talents) by protecting them from those who seek to exploit their talents for profitable gain.

One such construct is language and its use as an intelligence measuring tool in modern society or a predictor of how well a student will do in school. This tool has miscalculated that African Americans who don't score well on standardized tests will not do well in school. There is a myth that language is not valued in the African American culture. This could not be further from the truth! The African American culture has produced some of the most profound lyricists and celebrated orators known to modern man, including: Shawn Carter (Jay Z), Tupac Shakur, Sean Combs (P. Diddy) Dr. Martin Luther King Jr., Malcolm X, Reverends Jesse Jackson and Al Sharpton, and the infamous Louis Farrakhan. African American males who use their oratorical skills to play the dozens (talking about each other's mothers) or to "freestyle," (rapping about situations around them without practice), are sometimes categorized as trouble makers or misfits. While the dominant society mocks our boys calling rap misogynistic, gangster and immature, rap is being used in Mc Donald's commercials, online school commercials, cell phone advertisements and anything dealing with selling sportswear to the very children society seems to be mocking. Most recently a new way to learn the SAT vocabulary was introduced in rap called "FLOCABULARY," showing the importance of this part of African American culture and the relevance to ethnicity, self- esteem and education.

These verbal rituals take a great deal of skill, wit, verbal and mental agility, as well as a mastery of the environment and organization of "super intelligent" skills. Anyone who has ever tried to 'rap' knows it's difficult enough to practice, let alone free-styling (no practice) off the top of your head, while seeking to entertain the group and insulting your opponent in the process. Unfortunately, our young African American boys are not assessed on these attributes during standard measures of verbal intelligence. However, children of other ethnic backgrounds who demonstrate high verbal skills on the standard measuring tests are rewarded handsomely with scholarships, honors classes and a head held high with great self-esteem.

I have written this small work to arouse a different conversation amongst intellectuals, parents and educators. I hope this would affect a different kind of research orientation toward the education of African American males in this country. To my critics, I am not ostracizing African American girls, but many African American males are seemingly being wiped out of mainstream society, while others are ostensibly being lured into the world of rap and/or athletic endeavors. While being a former athlete and grasping the value of sports, I also realize that we need a larger number of African American children to understand that they have a multitude of talents that extend beyond the world of entertainment.

A Call to Reason; Losing our Manhood

With the advent of the Brown vs. Board of Education decision in 1954, Dr. Martin Luther King sought to release African Americans from the Pharaohs (political exploiters), the "Hamans" (religious intellectual exploiters), and the "Quroons" (economic exploiters of the poor and destitute). However, after his death there are thousands more alive and well, thriving in the inner cities waiting for the next Kobe Bryant, Kevin Garnett or Lebron James. *The people who were destined to be the best community brought out for humankind, the torchbearers, the peacemakers and the enlightened of civilization are now the laughing stock of the world.* African American males as a group seem to be the least respected group because of their estrangement and backwardness in a global world that has seemingly left them behind in technology, science and the modernity to a lowly position of helplessness and ignominy.

It is very important that the African American community be aware of these observable facts because many parents and guardians are so concerned with everyday life, that they are not aware our Black males are dropping out of the public schools at an unprecedented rate. The majority of African Americans depend on public schools as their life line to a better life and equality in a world that seems to only raise its eyebrows to the uneducated based prejudices and stereotypes. These stereotypes have been persistent for generations and are seemingly getting stronger as time goes on. These aforementioned facts are equally important to parents because awareness of the growing achievement gap between Black and White children, Asian and Black children and also Hispanic and Black children are growing and presently African American children are still at the bottom in all categories.

Chapter 2

Education Could Mean Life or Death!

Why do we raise this issue? The question of education for Black people in America is a question of life and death. It is a political question, a question of power... Struggle is a form of education-Perhaps the highest form.
-Lerone Bennett

The American education system has not been effective in educating Black children especially when it comes to African-American males. Traditional education has molded African-American children to ensure they fit into an education model for Anglo-Saxon middle class children. We know the system needs to be overhauled because a disproportionate number of African American children are being special-edized, drugged, suspended, expelled and or pushed out of schools at a rapid rate. This has led to an overrepresentation of African-American males in prison and a rising unemployment rate and I dare say overrepresentation of African American males in the military. As mentioned above, the excessive number of African-American children given drugs as tranquilizers, being labeled mentally retarded and placed in special education classes needs our attention ASAP. The numbers conclude that the system is failing because throughout the 1990's, the national college dropout rate for African-Americans was 20 to 25%

higher than that of Whites. Moreover, the college drop-out rate for African-Americans has risen 63% since the 1980s.

African-Americans who did finish college had on average a grade point average two-thirds lower than Whites. African-American males currently comprise the largest population of academic underachievers in the United States (Janssen, & Carton, 1999). There are studies that show African-Americans have progressed but continue to lag academically behind Whites (Okech, & Harrington, R. 2002; 1998; Killeya, 2001; Janssen, & Carton, 1999). As a result of the negative outcomes associated with the underachievement of the African-American male, researchers began to examine reasons for this lack of achievement (Lan, & Lanthier, R.2003). With high attrition rates and soaring costs because of the need to create remedial courses, colleges are searching for an answer to their dilemma of what makes a college student motivated and successful. A number of different theoretical constructs have been developed in order to seek an answer to this question. Researchers have considered a variety of mitigating factors that place African-American males in high risk categories for academic failure. Few studies have adequately explored socio-cognitive constructs of the effects of locus of control, self-esteem and self-efficacy of male African-American military student on achievement outcomes (Dollinger, 2000).

Locus of Control, Self-Esteem and Self-Efficacy

Rotter (1966) defined internal locus of control as one who believes that whatever happens in life occurs because of their own behavior and skills. The external locus of control takes the opposing view and is defined as someone who believes that life is "controlled by forces other than one's self" (Ayalon & Young, 2005). Studies have also shown that internals and externals "differ in numerous ways, particularly in terms of their cognitive activity and environmental mastery" (Dollinger, 2000).

Almost as soon as the locus of control construct was conceptualized, researchers began to apply it to education. In 1966, in a report on Equality in Educational Opportunity, it was stated that students with a measured high level of internal locus of control performed better in school, while "external locus of control correlated to lower academic achievement and higher dropout rates." In a literature review conducted by Findley and Cooper (in Gifford & Bricelo-Perriot, et. al., 2006), it was found that "locus of control and academic achievement are significantly and positively related and that the magnitude of the relationship is small to medium" (Gifford & Bricelo-Perriot, et. al., 2006). Rayle & Arredondo (2005) maintained that an internal locus of control orientation could be changed through education.

When looking at reasons behind this, researchers have argued that African-American students are slow to develop internal locus of control, as a result of their past educational history and social background, *as opposed to both of which may have been overly shaped by external factors that seemed arbitrary and out of control by the students* (Hillman, Wood, and Sawilowsky, 1994). In order for any school to counteract the forces leading to external locus of control in African-American students, mentoring and programming must be developed which addresses each problem area and slowly demonstrates to the student that effort leads to success.

According to Bandura (1977), self-efficacy, self-esteem and locus of control are the *perceived abilities* to cope with specific situations and achieve identified goals. Recent studies have shown a direct relationship between a student's belief structure and behavior that suggest that self-efficacy and locus of control could be an important focus for cognitive intervention (Hall & Spruill, et. al., 2002). Bandura (1986) argued that cognitive intervention can work because self-efficacy, self-esteem and locus of control can improve one's confidence in one's own ability. It also makes one trust his or her environment. Individuals with higher levels of self-efficacy, self-esteem and locus of control are more motivated to stay focused on their desired goal until it is achieved. Bandura (1986) maintained that the most effective intervention is an improved sense of self–efficacy, self-esteem and locus of control. He explained that in order to increase academic achievement outcomes, one must begin by trusting one's environment and changes in behavior. On the basis of such findings, numerous educational reformers have argued that the best way to improve minority students' achievement is to improve their self-esteem, self-efficacy and locus of control, and that "increasing these constructs are indispensable to subsequent school learning" (Hillman, Wood, and Sawilowsky, 1994; Steele and Aronson, 1995; Aronson and Inzlicht, 2004; Okech and Harrington, 2002). There is a large amount of literature that suggests self-esteem, self-efficacy and locus of control can be improved if fostered in the right environment (Rubie & Townsend, et. al., 2002).

Gifford & Bricelo-Perriot (2006) argued that students with educators who foster the right environment of intervention strategies such as tutoring and mentoring showed significant increase in self-efficacy, self-esteem, locus of control and academic achievement levels. Congruent with these findings, researchers have argued that low self-esteem, low self-efficacy and a *stronger* locus of control in minority students can be reversed if the culture shock of the environment (school) is reduced (Rubie, Townsend, and Moore, 2004). The "military classroom (leadership schools) curricula has been described as interdisciplinary by nature, and demands a soldier have these constructs to be a leader" (Raviv, 2004).

Most minority students develop low self-esteem, low self-efficacy and weak locus of control as a result of ***culturally insensitive schooling***. Following these findings, if African-

American students believe that the assessing figure or instrument is prejudicial or discriminatory they will dis-identify with the negative assessment, often dangerously falling into the social mirror of a peer group that praises their inadequate performance, leading to learned helplessness.

African-American male college students who were polled said they continue to struggle through a system that they increasingly see as being "fixed" in favor of Anglo-Saxon students. The internal sense of locus of control they had as freshmen begins to convert to external locus of control, which has been overwhelmingly linked to poor academic achievement (Aronson & Inzlicht, 2004). Therefore, if more "culturally relevant teaching" was conducted, then their self-esteem would improve (Rubie & Townsend, et. al., 2004).

In conclusion, the research suggests that locus of control; self-efficacy and self-esteem can be learned through careful consideration of one's environment. The challenge to contemporary educators is to find ways to understand how large of a factor environment and culturally relevant teaching could play in the development of self-esteem and self-efficacy. That challenge includes finding out if those factors could lead to a higher sense of locus of control and self identification. My theory is that this would lead to better academic outcomes. The hypothesis of this work consists in the thought that to adequately teach a child, one must understand his psychological, social, as well as personal and emotional processes to ensure that the child will be successful. This is a formidable challenge and a huge responsibility for our already overworked and underpaid teachers.

CHAPTER 3

Does a Student's Belief Matter?

If a student believes they are not competent, then they will avoid challenges in order to protect their self-esteem. If, however, the student has high self-efficacy, they "will engage with challenging tasks whose successful accomplishment enhances feelings of pride and self-esteem.

-Rubie & Townsend, 2004

Okech & Harrington (2002), suggest that Western social scientists have a very myopic concept of what intelligence, self esteem, locus of control and self efficacy are. Along with these authors, a number of other studies "indicate that there may be differences in psychological functioning and behaviors of African-Americans possessing different degrees of Black consciousness" (Okech & Harrington, 2002, p.34).

This book should be seen as a work in progress, a multidisciplinary work that draws upon many typical theories, as well as the most successful radical theories to help in this crisis of the African American male. While in the midst of a recession, the President of the United States (using an executive decision) was backed by Congress and the American people in a decision to write a big check to ensure that our bottom line was stable. This was done so our country would not go under. This work is focused as a cry for a bail out of men who are being lost in a system that appears to have no regard for their well being. Many believe that if they simply pull themselves up by their boots straps and work hard success will follow, since opportunity is all around. While opportunity is all around, an overwhelming amount of these young men are without" boot straps", and are sometimes so discouraged by the time they reach the 5th grade, they feel they are destined to walk bare foot for the rest of their lives. By this point in their lives, they have been labeled, ostracized and/or told that they cannot achieve success outside the sports world. In our society, a label such as 'inferior cognitive capability' is used to define African-American children because of poor reading skills or low achievement scores. My proposition is that we must create an educational system that not only celebrates African Americans during the month of February but also provides them daily with the survival skills needed to contribute in meaningful ways to ensure proper self-esteem and locus of control. When White middle class children have less than desirable reading achievement, it is seldom suggested the defect lies within the child but rather the method of instruction itself. The question at hand is how and what does this accomplish for the self-esteem of the White child and by juxtaposition what on the other hand does it do for the self-esteem of the African American child?

> *If a student believes they are not competent, then they will avoid challenges in order to protect their self-esteem. If, however, the student has high self-efficacy, they "will engage with challenging tasks whose successful accomplishment enhances feelings of pride and self-esteem" (Rubie & Townsend, et. al., 2004).*

Socio-cognitive conceptualizations of the self as they apply to the achievement of high school and college students have been examined in general (Van Laar, 2000). Most studies involving these psychological constructs, locus of control, self-esteem and self-efficacy have focused on academic settings and have examined these constructs separately or in pairs on middle school, high school and college students. Of twenty-three articles reviewed, thirteen focused on primary and secondary education levels. All articles included White students, six included Hispanic students and five included African-Americans in their sample populations. In only three of these studies were all three ethnicities included; three examined Whites and Hispanics, and two examined Whites and African-Americans. Within the White only populations of the studies, seven included both male and female; two of the studies were male only and four studies were female only.

Of the same twenty-three articles reviewed, eight focused on college students -- six examined undergraduates and two examined graduate students. Both of the graduate studies and three of the six undergraduate studies included African-Americans, Hispanics, and Whites in their populations. Only one undergraduate study compared African-Americans to Whites. Another undergraduate study included only African-Americans and the remaining study included only Whites. Both of the graduate studies and three of the undergraduate studies included both males and females. Two of the remaining three undergraduate studies were male only and one study was female only. Four of the college studies examined one construct only, three studied locus of control, and one studied self-efficacy. Three studies examined two constructs: two focused on locus of control and self-esteem, and one other on locus of control and self-efficacy. Only three of the college studies compared the constructs to academic achievement, and one compared the constructs with age.

While many studies have been published on self-efficacy, self-esteem and locus of control, no studies were found to have investigated all three constructs at one time, or to have considered environments other than the educational environment. There was not a study that focused on the African-American adult male student in the military. Furthermore, no study has compared civilian to military population of African-American males.

Open dialogue:

Is the Military the Solution?

As mentioned above there seems to be an overrepresentation of African American males in the military and a growing number of African American females joining because of a variety of reasons mainly the economy and the perceived equity in the armed services for upward mobility. I believe the African-American community has a love hate relationship with the military. On the record, most African-Americans I interviewed about their reasons for joining the military said it was because they loved their country and wanted to defend its honor, while off the record, their reasons are economically driven. By having a steady job with enormous medical and educational benefits, it's a means to an end for many of them. In over 200 interviews of African American males in uniform, 85 percent said it was a job that gave them not only a career but an opportunity for education and to be looked at favorably not only by family but the larger society. This led me to look at African-Americans like myself, who came into the military for a better life, discipline and education. While I too fall in the 85 percent of who came in for those above mentioned reasons, eventually most of us began to believe in the call to patriotism as a parallel to our original goals.

That being said I wanted to look into the profession of arms in which I have served for the last 18 years as an option for African American males. I rose up the ranks from Private to Major with little effort beyond hard work and taking advantage of the opportunities presented to me. Why look at the military (environment) as a source of fortification for African American males? Although it may be seen as a culture of combat, confrontation and war, the military environment is one of great expectations and standards of excellence. After effortlessly moving up the ranks, I wondered if I was an abnormality, an aberration or was this common trend among African American males who chose the military as a way of life. Indeed we all know of Colin Powell, the Four Star General who became Chairman of the Joint Chiefs of Staff and was the first African American appointed as Secretary of State. I have sparingly seen a couple of other Black Generals in the Army, but I was more intrigued with what I saw on an everyday level. What I saw included African-American men in charge on the enlisted side of the house at every rank from first year Sergeant to Command Sergeant Major of the Army. I thought this was amazing because at every duty station where I was assigned there were Black men in charge at the highest levels of the enlisted ranks. While in my 18 years I have served in only two units commanded by African American Colonels, I have served in numerous units with African American sergeant majors. As a matter of fact ninety nine percent of the sergeant majors were African American.

    Because of the pride, tenacity and confidence I witnessed in these exceptional men (one woman) I served with, I wanted to measure how the military environment aided in the development of their self-esteem, and self-efficacy. Secondly, I wanted to know if their sense of pride was connected to belief that the military provided equal opportunity when it came to promotion of African American males.

> *A senior Army official was quoted on the internet as saying "Doing affirmative action the right way is deadly serious for us—people's lives depend on it." He went on to say in this interview that racial diversity was necessary to ensure national security because to fight effectively, Soldiers needed to be a cohesive fighting force to be successful.*

The official quoted above is correct in that the Army has always led the way and has been the most courageous of all the services in its upfront attitude to racial integration starting in the 1960s and 1970s. Although this book is not about the military in particular, it nevertheless discusses the military environment and how it fosters self-esteem and self-efficacy while giving all its Soldiers a sense of locus of control based upon standards of excellence.

Since the 1948 abolishment of segregation by President Truman, the military has always allowed African-Americans Soldiers to co-exist and fight among its Caucasian American Soldiers. Although, one can assume that all racial problems have not gone away, there does seem to be a sense of fairness about opportunities for advancement in the Army in which I serve. A study by Brink and Louis in the early 1960's concurred with my assessment that African Americans, even in historical times, "perceived" the military as a place with a better chance for equalitarian leadership training and promotion up the ladder of success, as opposed to the larger civilian society. Does this translate into a culture of transcendence for the African American male? Is this an environment of equality where African Americans can feel a sense of locus of control, where their self-esteem and self-efficacy can be strengthened because of the opportunities to be 'in charge' and lead those from other ethnicities? Can this one example of a different environment help in producing a plan in helping with this apparently overwhelming problem of the failure among the population of African-American young men? If it is true that self-esteem can be directed or changed by the environment you are in, then different environments should not only be discussed they should be explored. Self-esteem and self-efficacy have been proven to be statistically significant in sports, which are essentially a different environment based upon some passion, love and a belief that African-American males have seen examples of success. Why is this important? It is important because belief is essential to success, self-esteem and self-efficacy. To reiterate the point again, Brink and Louis said that African Americans, even in historical times, "perceived" the military as a place with a better chance for equalitarian leadership training and promotion up the ladder of success, as opposed to the larger civilian society. Today this is still true in the hearts of African Americans. The perception is that if you work hard you will receive the deserved promotion. Secondly, you will also have an equal opportunity to excel in school which is provided to all service members.

> *** Remember**
>
> If a student believes they are not competent, then they will avoid challenges in order to protect their self-esteem. If, however, the student has high self-efficacy, they "will engage with challenging tasks whose successful accomplishment enhances feelings of pride and self-esteem" (Rubie & Townsend, et. al., 2004).

Chapter 4

Two Worlds Two Souls?

Can environment affect cognition?

The negro is sort of a seventh son, born with a veil, and gifted with second sight in this American world- a world which yields him no true consciousness, but only lets him see himself through the revelation of the other world…. One never feels his two-ness as a American, a negro two souls, thoughts unreconciled strivings; two ideas in one dark body, whose dogged strength alone keeps it from being torn asunder.

-W. E. B. Dubois

W. E. B. Dubois's description of the African-American is disturbing, but also true as he describes African Americans as having two "warring souls." One shaped and nurtured by the Caucasian-American culture and the other by an innate Afro-American culture and we are expected to show loyalty to both. If we show disloyalty to the Caucasian-American culture we are branded as un-patriotic. Yet, if we are disloyal to the Afro-American culture we will have our "Black Card" revoked and be pronounced Uppity, Bourgeoisie, Uncle Tom or even worse a Sellout. Both are frightening possibilities in that we want to belong to both, as we are products of both. As an Officer in the United States Army and an African-American male, I have faced similar situations. You would like to choose a middle ground which is the correct course of action in all aspects of life, but most times you are in a position where one foot is on land and the other is on water. In any situation where you are becoming acclimated into a new culture, it is imperative that you do the best you can to fit into the dominate culture. Within the military, the officer rankings are strongly populated by White males. This group has its own cultural aspects and demands, which differ tremendously from the enlisted ranks, where the largest numbers of African American males reside. Where do I fall? Where do I lay my head? Where is my safe haven? Along with many African-Americans, I am trapped in between two worlds and we all try our best to navigate to dry land without being persecuted by either group.

Environment and Ethnicity

Considerable attention has been given in literature to culture (environment) and cognition. Although the term culture evolved in the 20th century into a definition almost always linked to anthropology, in its inception it was linked to an integrated pattern of human knowledge, belief and behavior, a shared set of goals, values and practices in an organization or a group. For the purpose of this work we will insist on the word 'culture' as environment (shared set of goals).

Havighurst (1976) said within complex society ethnic groups and social classes have two functions: production of diversity in human life style and development. Each group has separate attitudes and behaviors that distinguish it from the other social classes (p.56). He goes a little further by stating environmental patterns are transmitted (socializations occur) within social classes and ethnic groups through the same mechanisms: family, peer groups, common literature, formal associations and residential segregation (p.57). Thus these types of forces set in motion develop human behavior within the context of its ethnicity, always readily explaining what couldn't be understood by social class considerations alone.

Although these constructs have emerged in research in a variety of ways, the research has increasingly revealed that self-esteem, self-efficacy and locus of control are interactive in complex ways dependent on age, environment and ethnicity. As a result of the emergence of the socio-cognitive approach to exploring college students, a wave of studies on student self-esteem, self-efficacy and locus of control have been conducted in the last decade (Rubie & Townsend, 2004). Most researchers have failed to take age, environment and ethnicity into clearly defined consideration because of complexities in the process of conceptualizing how self-esteem, self-efficacy and locus of control interact.

S.B. Sarason (1983) suggests that educators must consider that one's attitudes are shaped by their particular environment and ethnic culture. He goes on to describe Blackness and Jewishness as descriptions of people who have Jewish and African American ethnicity. People who are socialized in those cultures are imbued with attitudes and characteristics that are rooted in history. He states these attitudes are like "second nature," learned, absorbed and inculcated into the process of cultural transmission" (p.965). Lastly, he states it is impossible to understand and evaluate each group's attitudes toward such activity. However, as mentioned in Chapter Two African-American males have done well in the military because of their positive attitude and sustained hope for continued equality and the opportunity for greater education and promotional opportunities. Sarason and Havighurst (1983) were harmonious in their statements, although said in different ways. They both felt that culture and environment have played and will continue to play a significant role in the lives of people. If the environment is conducive to equality and fairness, it is likely people will be able to express their individuality and still be productive members in the environment. In my opinion, the military has shown itself to be a culture within a culture, and its participants refer to themselves as a colorless unit, one family based upon a common mission and that is to defeat the enemy. This type of uniformed attitudinal thinking led me to believe this type of environment helps in the development of self-esteem, self-efficacy and locus of control in African American males.

Studies show that most African-Americans start out college optimistically "believing they can overcome the barriers they face in society" (Van Laar, 2000). In a study of their attributional style upon entering college, most freshmen believe that they are in college because they worked hard. However, African-American students are also found to become "more pessimistic about their prospects as they go through college" and, it is conjectured, as they witness institutional and social barriers that appear to decide their fate, they come to attribute their failure to outside forces (Van Laar, 2000). On the basis of this perception, it is assumed that African-American college students may exhibit internal locus of control, positively related to achievement, when they arrive at college. However, they gradually switch to external locus of control associated with failure. Additionally, the study showed that African-American college students shift toward an external attribution of success or failure not because their sense of self-worth and self-esteem has been eroded by college life, but as part of a cognitive strategy designed to protect their self-esteem as they move through college (Van Laar, 2000).

Regardless, research continues to examine ultimate sources of difficulty in higher education as they relate to these three constructs. This area of research has regained a sense of urgency, as trends among African-American college students have again begun to exhibit increasingly disturbing results (Van Laar, 2000). While the number of African-Americans enrolled in higher education increased by 40% between 1974 and 1984, over the last fifteen years, "there has been a leveling off in the number of African-American college students" even as the number of White students continues to grow (Van Laar, 2000). Moreover, even when African-American students arrive at college the attrition rate among this demographic stands at an alarming 62%, compared to 40% for all college students (Van Laar, 2000). One finding has important repercussions, if true. If African-American students believe that the assessing figure or instrument is prejudicial or discriminatory then they tend to dis-identify with the negative assessment, often dangerously falling into the social mirror of a peer group that praises their inadequate performance, leading to learned helplessness. Consequently, apply this finding to the college African-American male struggling through a system that he feels is a "fixed environment" in favor of White students, then whatever internal sense of locus of control he had as a freshman would convert to external locus of control, which has been overwhelmingly linked to poor academic achievement (Cassidy & Eachus, 2000; Dollinger, 2000).

As a result, researchers have begun to look more closely into the internal machinery of the student's mind in order to find out why some college students succeed and others do not. It is no longer enough to simply concede that one student is smart, and the other is not. Currently, researchers are exploring the hypothesis that a prime reason for the achievement gap lies in the student's mental and emotional makeup. Studies reveal that African-American male college students generally have external locus of control, even though they may enter college with a stronger sense of self. They do not believe that they are in control of their destiny, and more often than not blame external sources for their difficulties (Ayalon & Young, 2005; Cassidy & Eachus,

> If African-American students believe that the assessing figure or instrument is prejudicial or discriminatory then they tend to dis-identify with the negative assessment, often dangerously falling into the social mirror of a peer group that praises their inadequate performance, leading to learned helplessness.

2000; Dollinger, 2000; Flowers & Milner, et. al., 2003; Moneta & Schneider, et. al., 2001; Park & Kim, 1998; Pokrajac-Bulian & Zivcic-Becirevik, 2005; Shelley & Pakenham, 2004; Twenge & Zhang, et. al., 2004; Van Laar, 2000).

One response to this direction of the studies has been to seek a more holistic approach. How best does one study a student's success in complicated relationships between intellectual and emotional factors? A socio-cognitive system approach has been developed to examine the underlying factors that contribute to a student's success (Rubie & Townsend, 2004). The "large socio-cognitive system ...acts to organize, guide and regulate achievement behavior" in a student (Rubie & Townsend, 2004). This system of personal agency contains a number of constructs which determine whether or not a student thinks he or she is able to achieve good grades and has the internal drive that makes them aware that success must come from personal effort. The primary constructs in which research has been derived are self-esteem, self-efficacy, and expectations of success and locus of control. Overall, "students with high self-efficacy enter learning situations believing they can be successful, and they bring to bear all the resources they have to accomplish this learning (Rubie & Townsend, 2004).

The importance of this construct is based on the finding that a student's beliefs about their abilities are more important than their actual ability level, in terms of achieving good academic results. If a student believes they are not competent, they will avoid challenges in order to protect their self-esteem. However, if the student has high self-efficacy, they "will engage with challenging tasks whose successful accomplishment enhances feelings of pride and self-esteem" (Rubie & Townsend, et. al., 2004).

A question can be raised on what effect environment may play. All studies to date focus on one type of environment, the public school system or public universities. However, other contexts do exist where the population of African-American males is high and would seemingly be a fine environment to include in the holistic approach, the military and or military student in civilian school environments. In the context of military leadership schooling, the mechanism of self-esteem and locus of control may be expected to be less challenging than in the civilian context. It is a standard assumption and expectation that military-oriented youth are much more highly motivated and have received more explicit support from family, due to the dramatic nature of this particular career choice (Boyd, 2000). Moreover, most "students" in the military context have an interest in promotional opportunities which may mean that they have enrolled in civilian classes in order to achieve a more explicit and clear-cut goal. It is also less likely that peer group pressure in the military context will be operationalized in the negative manner as described by Hillman & Wood (1994) in their classic study on learned helplessness. The pre-training of military personnel as such would appear to preclude this possibility. The fact that by and large the military profession is a vocation, and that soldier-students are returning to class after training in the field, would also seem to imply that by profession the military person has a stronger locus of control. That said ranking may be a factor as would the determination of whether or not the student continues to favor military life (Hillman & Wood (1999).

Overall, the dramatic rise in African-American dropout rates in high school and through college leaves a precipitous set of options before young African-American males trying to make their way in the world into adulthood and calls into question the prior research. Despite the seemingly solid findings in studies that focus on Whites, the jury is still out on singular and combined impact that environment and age have on the development of locus of control, self-efficacy and self-esteem in African-American males to their peers and what impact these have on achievement in general and on academic achievement specifically.

In support of both theories, a study found that a student can be helped in changing from an external to an internal locus of control. This is accomplished often by simply finding ways to help him or her "enjoys learning and realizes that competence improves through their own efforts." The advantage of this approach to locus of control, self-efficacy and self-esteem is that in addition to exposing a myth, it situates these variables in the context of a societal struggle, indirectly related to stages of consciousness and fluctuations of the barometric self. If students can be trained to believe in themselves and see that effort leads to positive outcomes, then they can be led to develop a more internal locus of control (Hall & Spruill, et. al., 2002).

The conceptual framework in Figure 1 shows the final study predictors and dependent variable of academic achievement. Academic achievement is measured by environments of Military, Afrocentric vs. Non-Afrocentric. Based on the Theory of Social Learning, we would expect to see differences by environment and Afrocentric and/or Non-Afrocentric education on the academic achievement outcomes as they relate to these three measures of self-esteem, self-efficacy, and locus of control.

Figure 1. Conceptual Framework – Constructs and Measures

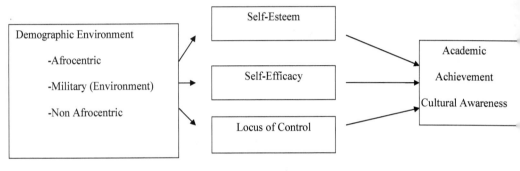

Hypotheses:

The first two hypotheses are related to Research Question 1. The third hypothesis is related to Research Question 2 and the last hypothesis is related to Research Question 3.

H1. Environment has no effect on the student's self-esteem, self-efficacy, and locus of control.   a. Environment has no effect on the student's self-esteem

b. Environment has no effect on the student's self-efficacy

c. Environment has no effect on the student's locus of control.

H2. Non Afrocentricity/ Afrocentricity have no effect on the student's self-esteem, self-efficacy, and locus of control.

a. Afrocentricity has no effect on the student's self-esteem

b. Afrocentricity has no effect on the student's self-efficacy

c. Afrocentricity has no effect on the student's locus of control

H3. Military has no effect on the student's ethnicity, self-esteem; self-efficacy and locus of control do not contribute to student's academic achievement.

CHAPTER 5

Afrocentric vs. Non Afrocentric Education
Which theory is most effective?

MULTI-DISCIPLINARY APPROACHES

The objective of this study is to determine if different environments have an impact on African American males' locus of control, self-esteem and self-efficacy, in their life as well as academic achievement. There has been little scholarly research to date on the comparative use of environment on these constructs that address African-American males. Additional research studies are needed.

The information gained can be used to provide further insight into the plight of African-American males, and may provide better understanding on environmental conditions that contribute to higher levels of all constructs. This chapter will discuss the nature and scope of this approach, to determine if it would help or hinder in the fortification of African American males and the improvement of their self-esteem and or self-efficacy. Researchers have called for innovative culturally responsive programs to enhance Black males' academic achievement. The Benjamin E. Mays Institute (BEMI) seeks to build on the idea of an Afrocentric model that proposes modeling, emphasizes cultural strengths and pride, and single sex instruction as opposed to a dual sex environment. He takes this approach with Afrocentric groups and Non-

Afrocentric groups. Mays sampled sixty-one middle school Black males and the results revealed that students had significantly greater academic attachment scores and academic success as opposed to their non-Afrocentric control group.

Afrocentric vs. Non-Afrocentric Education

Many of the principles in this theory of Afrocentric education were established by Carter G. Woodson in his book, *The Mis-Education of the Negro* (1933). He argues what the fundamental problems are pertaining to the education of African persons in America. He goes on to say that African Americans have been educated away from their culture and traditions and attached their lifestyle to the European culture; which dislocates them from themselves. Woodson also asserts that African Americans often valorize European culture to the defilement of their own culture and heritage (p.7). An interesting point to note is that Woodson didn't advocate a rejection of American national values; however he believed that African Americans should uplift and uphold their own values and traditions or this type of mentality would assure cultural and psychological death. Furthermore, he argued, if education is to be substantial within the African American experience it must first address African American experiences in America and Africa (p.7).

Ronald Ferguson (2002) concurred with the above sentiments by saying when African American students feel supported, cared for and encouraged they are more likely to survive in school. Fifteen urban schools districts known for their academic success surveyed White, Black and Hispanic students and found that when African American students were in a supportive and encouraging environment they succeeded and worked harder than their counterparts. Is this important? Can these findings lead to a different approach to dealing with African American males in education?

Kwame Agyei Akoto (2002) details what he thinks is Afrocentric education, which he terms "Afrikan" centered education. He argues that it is rooted in the unique history that evolved from African people. Below he gives a list of what he formulated as essential for the growth of African American males:

- A commitment to African history and culture and the solidarity of the African identity.
- A focus on the origins, current status and future of the African World.
- A commitment to correcting historical distortions.
- A concern for developing students with an African nationality within the educational system.
- The ability to projects a humanist and pluralistic viewpoint of afro-centricity as a valid non-controlling perspective.
- Lastly, the ultimate goal is to de-program and ensure Black males who have been mis-educated in their current system, and to prevent the cultural negation of future generations of African Americans.

Dr. Ramona H. Enderlin (1996) argues that Afrocentric education is at this point the only process that can bring out the genius in our children. She says African centered education allows African American males to see themselves as people, as opposed to subjects and as participants in human activity and history. Dr. Enderlin goes on to say, that tapping into the soul of our children is to be found outside the classroom (Hilliard, Payton-Stewart and Williams, pg.37).

Dr. Wade Nobles concurred and added his point of view on additional goals of African centered education. He said that African centered education should develop our children in competence, confidence and consciousness (Hilliard, Payton-Stewart and Williams, pg.37).

Children should not only exhibit positive attitudes but be able to demonstrate their abilities with purpose in life through strong character and high achievement.

Historically, sociologically, and educationally, Afrocentric education has focused on the relationship between students and teachers. Is this important for student achievement? Yes, because not only does it develop trust, it also develops a sense of high expectations from those you care about. Many teachers from the Afrocentric educational perspective saw themselves having similar lives and experiences as the students for whom they were responsible. This level of care turned into more of a paternal role of mother and or fatherly relationship in which the student now had their own expectation to succeed because of the relationship.

Societal Expectations

Opposing views to the aforementioned Afrocentric education at the beginning of the 20th century asserted that the culture of African Americans actually contributes a significant role in the low achievement of the community. In his book "Losing the Race: Self-Sabotage in Black America," John McWhorter argued that African American cultural *traits... because* they embrace forces such as anti intellectualism. In this study, he seemed to overlook such systematic forces like racism, discrimination and disproportionate poverty. His findings are discredited by contemporary models of African American success in some schools. He based his findings on students that attended his classes on the campus of The University of California Berkley.

Abigail and Stephan Thernston, in their book "No Excuses: Closing the Racial Gap in Learning," determined that a great deal of under achievement, even within affluent African-American environments was due to low effort and low expectations by the students, as well as parents.

In his book, "Black American Students in an Affluent Suburb: A study of academic Disengagement," Ogbu concluded that attending schools that are predominately populated by affluent Whites does not exclude and/or mitigate discriminative practices that adversely impact the negative self-esteem of African American students. Theresa Perry, Asa Hilliard and Claude Steele are all African-American scholars that also concluded that structural forces within these school districts and schools can hinder academic achievement of African American students (i.e., policies and practices, teachers' expectation, etc). These scholars also argued that substantial analysis of the socialization engagement of students with other class mates and or teachers also factor into self- esteem and academic achievement.

Teacher Expectations

Dr. Janice Hale-Benson and Barbara Shade (2004), assert that institutional strategies in the current educational system has consistently failed African American students because teacher's expectations for African American males are sometimes linked to the images that are portrayed by the larger society of African American males being thugs, clowns, buffoons and/or drug dealers. They emphasize the need to re-educate the teachers by creating different mindsets that are conducive to the overall well being of African-American males to achieve academic success.

In addition, other scholars also believe that a teacher's expectation is a key determinant of student learning. Teacher's expectations of students have been known to shape student learning and achievement. Proponents of this paradigm note that educators create a self-fulfilling prophecy into students from diverse and or different racial backgrounds. Dr. Ramona H. Enderlin (1996) says that a teacher's expectations directly affect a student's self-esteem and academic achievement, which could have poisonous consequences for students learning to navigate through life. She goes on to say that when a teacher destroys a child's view of success by not expecting them to succeed, that teacher denies them access to the unlimited knowledge and resources the world has to offer, essentially killing the child before he/she can mature into self-efficacy (p.78)

African-American and Hispanic students have disproportionate structural inequalities by being placed on lower academic tracks in comparison to their White and Asian counterparts and therefore experience lower academic achievement and have lower prospects for college. Jamal Braddock and Jeannie Oakes (1995) noted how structures within schools reproduce social inequalities by tracking African Americans students to lower-level academic courses which in turn continue to influence disparities in achievement among this demographic.

In conclusion, while all research should be considered, according to cultural theorists the above reasoning does not adequately explain why some African-Americans achieve and others underachieve. They also concluded that schools should take into consideration culture of the minority groups because it could, based on research, help the self-esteem and self-efficacy of the displaced group.

Chapter 6

Stereotype Threat

In the early 1980's, Ogbu materialized as one of the most influential critics of cultural difference theory. Ogbu (1983) was critical of educational anthropologist who conducted cultural mismatch studies which reduced to de-contextualized practices. Ogbu argued that culture as a conceptualization was a "lived experience" which combined ecological and historical. He went on to say power had a huge effect on minorities and could explain the failure of some minority groups.

Having examined data of achievement for African Americans and other countries, Ogbu found that being a racial minority and having a different culture in itself does not predict school failure. For example Native Americans, African Americans and Hispanic Americans experience disproportionate school failure in the United States, but Japanese Americans, Chinese Americans and Filipinos do not. Ogbu's 1983 study of school achievement among the six aforementioned ethic groups didn't allow him to conclude that being a part of a racial minority doesn't predict school performance. However, he did argue that group incorporation into the host society and the group's social position in the society could predict academic achievement.

Stereotype threat refers to being at risk of confirming self-characteristics and/or negative stereotype about one's group (Steele & Arsonson 1995). This term was first used in 1995 by Aronson and Steele, and later showed up in several experiments of Black college freshmen and sophomores who performed more poorly on standardized test than their White counterparts when their race was actually emphasized. This study showed that when race was highlighted, Black students performed at a below average rate. However, when race was not emphasized, they performed equally and/or better than White students. Stereotype threat has been confirmed in three hundred or more articles that Charita Hardison and Paul Sackett have written that find from stereotype threat; race plays a role in test scores and achievement gaps.

Katz, Roberts, and Robinson (1965) reported similar effects in their study. However, Steele and Aronson's renewed exploration brought new light on this important problem. They have conducted over 300 experiments to date, on this theory which have been published in peer-reviewed articles and journals (Nguyen & Ryan, 2008 and Walton & Cohen, 2003). Steele & Arsonson (1995) developed four ways to understand stereotype threat including consequences, determining who is most vulnerable, understanding situations and long term effects. Steele and Aronson believed consequences went beyond underachievement in the classroom. They argued that if a student perceives the stereotype threat it can reduce the rate in which an ethnic minority will pursue further education and or life goals (Aronson, et al. 2002; Osborne, 1995; Steele, 1997).

Who is most vulnerable to stereotype threat? Research has shown that academic performance of any individual who invokes this theory, based on expectation can be hurt. Stereotype threat has also been shown to affect other ethnic minorities like the Hispanics (Gonzales, Blanton, & Williams, 2002 Schmader& Johns, 2003) students from low socioeconomic backgrounds (Croizet & Claire, 1998), females in math (Good, Aronson & Harden, 2008), and Whites males when faced with the presence of Asian superiority in math (Aronson, Lustina, Good, Koegh, Steele& Brown 1999).

Marx & Staple (2006) explained situations that are most likely to lead to stereotype threat. Understanding situations, it should be noted that some members of any group may be more vulnerable to the negative effects of stereotype threat than others based on their particular circumstances. When one considers the possibility of negative stereotype, their performance can be undermined i.e. "I am African American and they expect me to bad on this SAT test anyway and this test is already difficult" One's performance can be undermined because of concerns of fulfilling the negative stereotype about the group being discriminated against. Therefore, the situation increases can increase the vulnerability of the stereotyped group to the threat.

Katz, Roberts, and Robinson (1965) believe that long term affects of stereotype threat may contribute to social inequality and furthermore this type of threat can be shown to affect individual's performance, life skills and a number of domains beyond academics such as White men in sports, women in negotiation (Kray, Galinsky, & Thompson, 2002), or homosexual men providing childcare (Bosson, Haymovitz, & Pinel, 2004).

If a student believes they are not competent, then they will avoid challenges in order to protect their self-esteem. If, however, the student has high self-efficacy, they "will engage with challenging tasks whose successful accomplishment enhances feelings of pride and self-esteem." I have again quoted this statement by Rubie & Townsend because this chapter dealt with this quote specifically. It proved without a shadow of a doubt, that when race was highlighted, Black students at a below average rate. However, when it was not they performed equally and or better than White students. So what happens to these students, who as the military say are "dropped from the role?" My theory is that they end up in the unemployment lines; they end up being men who can't provide for their families, so most give up on society as they "believe" that society has given up on them. Their final resting place becomes either in the garden of memories, the pits of hell or the penitentiary.

Chapter 7

Race and Prison

According to the US Census Bureau, the US population in 2000 was 281,421,906. Of that, 194,552,774 (69.1%) were White; 3,947,837 (12.1%) were Black; and 35,305,818 (12.5%) were of Hispanic origin. Additionally, 2,068,883 (0.7%) were Native American, and 10,123,169 (3.8%) were Asian (2007). At midyear 2007, the incarceration rate of Black women held in custody (prison or jail) was 348 per 100,000 U.S. residents compared to 146 Hispanic women and 95 White women. With the exception of females ages 55 to 59, black women were held in custody at higher rates than Hispanic or White women across all age categories.

William J. Sabol (2008) said "In 2001, the chances of going to prison were highest among Black males (32.2%) and Hispanic males (17.2%) and lowest among White males (5.9%)." Sabol also argued that because of their extraordinary rate of incarceration, one in every 20 Black men over the age of 18 is in a state or federal prison, compared to one in every 180 Whites." In five states, between one in 13 and one in 14 Black men are in prison. At the start of the 1990s, the U.S. had more Black men (between the ages of 20 and 29) under the control of the nation's criminal justice system than the total number in college. This and other factors have led some scholars to conclude that "crime control policies are a major contributor to the disruption of the family, the prevalence of single parent families, and children raised without a father in the ghetto, and the 'inability of people to get the jobs still available (p.11)." Similar to men in the general prison population (93%), parents held in the nation's prisons at midyear 2007 were mostly male (92%). More than 4 in 10 fathers were Black, about 3 in 10 were White, and about 2 in 10 were Hispanic. An estimated 1,559,200 children had a father in prison at midyear 2007; nearly half (46%) were children of Black fathers (Sabol, William J. 2008). "Thirteen percent of all adult Black men, a total of 1.4 million men, are disenfranchised, representing one-third of the total disenfranchised population and reflecting a rate of disenfranchisement that is seven times the national average. Election voting statistics offer an approximation of the political importance of Black disenfranchisement: 1.4 million Black men are disenfranchised compared to 4.6 million Black men who voted in 1996."

"African American males represented the largest percentage (35.4%) of inmates held in custody, followed by White males (32.9%) and Hispanic males (17.9%)."Over a third (33.8%) of the total male custody population was ages 20 to 29. The largest percentage of Black (35.5%) and Hispanic (39.9%) males held in custody were ages 20 to 29. White males ages 35 to 44 have accounted for the largest percentage (30.1%) of the White male custody population (p.7). Lauren E. Glaze and Laura Maruschak looked at statistics from the Department of Justice that indicated that Black males are incarcerated – held in prison or jail – at a rate that is over 6 times higher than that for White males. For every 100,000 Black males, an estimated 4,777 are held in federal or state prison or a local jail. By contrast, for every 100,000 White men, only 727 are estimated to be incarcerated.

Table 1

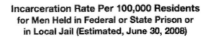

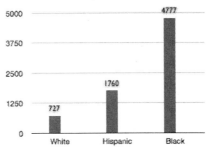

Source: Bureau of Justice Statistics, *Prison Inmates at Midyear 2008 – Statistical Tables,* March 2009 (Revised 4/8/09), Table 1

One result of this high incarceration rate is that the percentage of Blacks among all males in prison or jail far exceeds the percentage of Blacks in the general population:

	Percent in US Population	Percent in Prison, Jail
Whites	66%	34%
Blacks	13%	40%
Hispanics	15%	20%
Other	6%	6%

Calculated from Bureau of Justice Statistics, *Prison Inmates at Midyear 2008 – Statistical Tables,* March 2009 (Revised 4/8/09).

Conclusion and Community Questions

Looking at the last chapter, one can understand why there is a need to sound the alarm and seek ways to find any solution to help young African American males in failing school system. I believe there is a direct correlation between African Americans dropping out from school and a increased population in the prison system. While the limitations of this book don't prove that this is the case, common sense will provide the answers to some problems as opposed to research. The chances of a person dropping out of high school and maintaining a trouble free life seems highly unlikely to me but it's just an assumption on my part. Although this book doesn't cover it I wondered how self-esteem affected the African American male life that leads him to go to prison. Secondly how is his self-esteem while in prison? Because I am active duty military I neither had the time nor those resources to sample this population. So below I thought maybe someone could pick up the ball and write based on the questions below in my concluding paragraphs.

This book represents a multidiscipline approach to a problem that only seems to be getting worse month by month, and year by year. While this study is not giving solutions and has undoubtedly created more questions than answers, it is seeking to encourage educators to take a look at different ways to educate this deteriorating population.

- What are we to do?
- Is this a Black problem?
- Is this a societal problem?
- Is it a government problem?

- Do we pull ourselves up by our boot straps?
- Is it a community problem?
- Does racism play a role in academics?
- Is discrimination the determining factor for the decline of African American males?
- Should we march on Washington again?
- What will it accomplish?
- Have African American mothers loved our boys and raised our girls?
- Do African Americans have different learning styles than other ethnicities?
- Are African American males doing enough on their own behalf?
- Are African American parents involved enough in their son's life, education and life choices?
- Do we need more African American men as role models in the school system?
- With the high dropout rate of African American males in high school where will they come from?
- Should we hold the African American males in the NBA, NFL AND MLB accountable to be more involved in our son's lives?

While all these questions should be answered by each individual in their particular situations, these are questions that arose when trying to put together this important work. I have considered my particular situation and the decisions that I made as a young boy growing up without a father's everyday presence in my life. I think of the times in class where I wanted to learn however, it wasn't cool to be smart so I 'dumbed' myself down to ensure I could remain a part of the *"in crowd."* What if the teachers said I am not going to let you fail because I believe in you? Would that have helped? As opposed to, "all you think about is basketball, you are going to be too dumb to remember the plays if you don't shape up." I believe that teachers' expectations, a solid structured home, role models who look like you and professionals in your community, are all contributing factors in the overall well-being and academic achievement of African-American males. I hope this book serves as a tool to start the conversation. Lastly, although I speak about African-American males and their failure rate as opposed the success rate of White communities and/or White males I would hope that this book is not seen as a book that promotes ill will to that community. I hope it could be seen as a beacon of light and a cry for help to a community that is or that needs a community to help dig it out from its despair.

In conclusion Dr. Naim Akbar said there is a difference in male, boys and men. Dr. Akbar said males are only capable of sightseeing as reality moves by they watch it from a distance with a hand extended hoping for a handout. Boys he exclaimed have dreams; they think they wonder they build unreal worlds in their mind. He concluded the only men have visions and visions become reality and the basis for human excellence. In line with these statements a special note and gratitude must go to urban prep high school a charter school for African American males. This school is the first of its kind in the United States. The uniqueness of this school is not only that it's all African American males the uniqueness is in that 100 percent of its graduating seniors are eligible for college. This School is in line with the subject of this book and that is environment could have an effect on the self-esteem and self–efficacy of African American males. The founders of Urban Prep high school in Chicago are visionaries in the sense that they noticed the need for immediate specialized attention on this demographic and put their vision into action. The school and its founders have created a culture where their mantra is and I quote: *"Building a positive school culture is very important at Urban Prep as it helps promote positive self-esteem and high achievement. One way we foster a positive school culture is by holding our students accountable to live by the Urban Prep Creed which they recite each morning in Community".*

The Urban Prep Creed

We believe. We are the young men of Urban Prep. We are college bound. We are exceptional- not because we say it, but because we work hard at it. We will not falter in the face of any obstacle placed before us.

We are dedicated, committed and focused. We never succumb to mediocrity, uncertainty or fear. We never fail because we never give up. We make no excuses. We choose to live honestly, nonviolently and honorably.

We respect ourselves and, in doing so, respect all people. We have a future for which we are accountable. We have a responsibility to our families, community and world. We are our brothers' keepers. /We believe in ourselves.

Researchers have concluded as this work will conclude and that is, African American males in the right environment will engage with challenging tasks and become successful based upon their surroundings. This schools precedence is harmonious with the above researchers findings in that they have argued that low self-esteem, low self-efficacy and a stronger locus of control in minority students can be reversed if the culture shock of the environment (school) is reduced.

Gifford & Bricelo-Perriot (2006) said that students with educators who foster the right environment of intervention strategies such as tutoring and mentoring showed significant increase in self-efficacy, self-esteem, locus of control and academic achievement levels. This school's creed brings us back to the hypothesis of the book and that is if a student believes they are not competent, then they will avoid challenges in order to protect their self-esteem. However given the right environment and taught to believe in themselves they will excel not only in self-esteem, self efficacy but also achievement. This school has obviously fostered an environment of achievement, self-esteem and made these students believe in themselves. I hope this book will serve as conversation starter to the dreadful condition to our boys in the school system. I hope and pray that all ethnicities will look at the essence of this book and come together as a community to help this demographic recover from the debilitating numbers of failure of African American males. Lastly, although this work was specifically about African American males. I hope and pray that we all have the courage to reach across the aisle and be each other's keepers whether in the school system and or life in general. We are commissioned by God to uplift not destroy humanity.

Chaplain (CPT) Shabazz Invocation before deployment to Iraq 2007

Chaplain (CPT) Shabazz @Tigris River Chapel Taji Iraq 2007

Chaplain (CPT) Shabazz visiting with the coalition Ques @ Iraq 2006

Chaplain(CPT)Shabazz @Tactical Operation center Taji Iraq 2007

Chaplain (CPT) Shabazz Visiting CW3 Hines @ Motor pool in Iraq 2008

References

Aronson, J. & Inzlicht, M. (2004). The ups and downs of attribution ambiguity: Stereotype vulnerability and the academic self-knowledge of African American college students. *American Psychological Society,* 129-837.

Ayalon, L. & Young, M.A. (2005). Racial group differences in help-seeking behaviors. *The Journal of Social Psychology, 145,* 391-403.

Borman, G.D. & Overman, L.T. (2004). Academic resilience in mathematics among poor and minority students. *The Elementary School Journal, 104,* 177-197.

Boyd, C.E. (2000). Supportive parents often boost military career advancement. *The Black Collegian,* 110-114.

Brownlow, S. & Reasinger, R.D. (1998). Putting off until tomorrow what is better done today: Academic procrastination as a function of motivation toward college work. *Procrastination: Current Issues and New Directions,* 15-36.

Cassidy, S. & Eachus, P. (2000). Learning style, academic belief systems, self-report student proficiency and academic achievement in higher education. *Educational Psychology, 20,* 307-324.

Charles, C.Z. & Massey, D.S. (2003). How stereotypes sabotage minority students. *Chronicle of Higher Education, 49,* B10-B12.

Covin, R., Donovan, A. & Macintyre, P.D. (2003). The relationship between self-esteem and performance when information regarding others' performance is available. *The Journal of Social Psychology, 143,* 541-544.

Dollinger, S.J. (2000). Locus of control and incidental learning: an application to college student success. *College Student Journal, 34,* 537-541.

Downing, T.K.E. (2006). The use of humor when counseling African American college students. *Journal of Counseling & Development, 84,* 10-17.

El-Anzi, F.O. (2005). Academic achievement and its relationship with anxiety, self-esteem, optimism and pessimism in Kuwaiti students. *Social Behavior and Personality, 33,* 95-104.

Estrada, L., Dupoux, E. & Wolman, C. (2006). The relationship between locus of control and personal-emotional adjustment and social adjustment to college life in students with and without learning disabilities. *College Student Journal, 40,* 43-54.

Fazey, D.M. A. & Fazey, J. A. (2001). The potential for autonomy in learning perceptions of competence, motivation and locus of control in first-year undergraduate students. *Journal of the Society for Research into Higher Education,* 345-363.

Flowers, L.A., Milner, H.R. & Moore, J.L. (2003). Effects of locus of control on African American high school seniors' educational aspiration: Implications for preservice and service high school teachers and counselors. *High School Journal, 87,* 39-50.

Gifford, D.D., Bricelo-Perriott, J. & Mianzo, F. Locus of control: academic achievement and retention in a sample of university first-year students. *Journal of College Admission, Spring,* 19-28.

Hall, C.W. (2001). A measure of executive processing skills in college students. *College Student Journal, 35,* 442-451.

Hall, C.W., Spruill, K.L. & Webster, R.E. (2002). Motivational and attitudinal factors in college students with and without learning disabilities. *Learning Disabilities Quarterly, 25,* 20-29.

Harter, S. & Whitesell, N.R. (2003). Beyond the debate: why some adolescents report stable self-worth over time and situation, whereas others report changes in self-worth. *Journal of Personality, 71,* 1027-1060.

Hillman, S.B., Wood, P.C. & Sawilowsky, S.S. (1994). Attributional style of African-American adolescents. *Social Behavior and Personality, 22,* 165-176.

James, L.V. (2004). Enhancing psychosocial competence about Black women in college. *Social Work, 49,* 74-84.

James, K.A., Phelps, L. & Bross, A.L. (2001). Body dissatisfaction, drive for thinness, and self-esteem in African American college females. *Psychology in the Schools, 38,* 491-498.

Janssen, T. & Carton, J.S, (1999). The effects of locus of control and task difficulty on procrastination. *The Journal of Genetic Psychology, 16,* 436-442.

Killeya, L.A. (2001). Idiosyncratic role-elaboration, academic performance and adjustment among African-American and European-American male college student athletes. *College Student Journal, 35,* 87-95.

Lan, W., & Lanthier, R. (2003). Changes in students' academic performance and perceptions of school and self before dropping out of schools. *Journal of Education for Students Placed at Risk, 8,* 309-332.

Meyer, H. (2000). Classroom participation sought by soldier-students in Iraq. Community College Week, June 20, 3-5.

Moneta, G.B., Schneider, B. & Csikzentmihalyi, M. (2001). A longitudinal study of the self-concept and experiential components of self-worth and affect across adolescence. *Applied Developmental Science, 5,* 125-141.

Nelson, E. & Williams, C. (1999). Perceived academic workload and locus of control in college students. Research for Educational Reform, 9. 3-10.

Okech, A.P. & Harrington, R. (2002). The relationship among Black consciousness, self-esteem, and academic self-efficacy in African American men. *The Journal of Psychology, 136,* 214-224.

Park, Y-S. & Kim, U. (1998). Locus of control, attributional style, and academic achievement: Comparative analysis of Korean, Korean-Chinese, and Chinese students. *Asian Journal of Social Psychology, 1,* 191-208.

Phelps, R.E., Taylor, J.D. & Gerard, P.A. (2001). Cultural mistrust, ethnic identity, racial identity, and self-esteem among ethnically diverse Black university students. *Journal of Counseling and Development, 78,* 209-217.

Pokrajac-Bulian, A. & Zivcic-Becirevik, I. (2005). Locus of control and self-esteem as correlates of body dissatisfaction in Croatian university students. *European Eating Disorders Review, 13,* 54-60.

Rayle, A.D., Arredondo, P. & Kurpius, S.E.R. (2005). Educational self-efficacy of college women: implications for theory, research and practice. *Journal of Counseling & Development, 83*, 361-368.

Raviv, A. (2004). The dilemmas of combining military and academic studies: the Israeli experience. B*altic Defense Review, 12*, 7-16.

Rubie, C.M., Townsend, M.A.R. & Moore, D.W. (2004). Motivational and academic effects of cultural experiences for indigenous minority students in New Zealand. *Educational Psychology, 24*, 143-152.

Shelley, M. & Pakenham, K.I. (2004). External health locus of control and general self-efficacy: Moderators of emotional distress among university students. *Australian Journal of Psychology, 56*, 191-199.

Seo, D-C., Blair, E.H., Torabi, M.R. & Kaidahl, M.A. (2004). Lifestyle and perceptional changes among college students since September 11. *American Journal of Health Studies, 19*, 20-29.

Smith, C.E. & Hopkins, R. (2004). Mitigating the impact of stereotypes on academic performance: The effects of cultural identity and attributions for success among African American college students. The Western Journal of Black Studies, 28, 312-333.

Spanierman, L.B. (2002). Academic self-efficacy within a culture of modern racism: The case of Benita. *The Career Development Quarterly, 50,* 331-336.

Spencer, M.B., Noll, E., Stoltzfus, J. & Harpalani, V. (2001). Identity and school adjustment: revisiting the 'acting White' assumption. *Educational Psychologist, 36,* 21-30.

Twenge, J.M., Zhang, L., Im, C. (2004). It's beyond my control: A cross-temporal meta-analysis of increasing externality in locus of control, 1960-2002. Personality and Social Psychology Review, 8, 308-319.

Van Laar, C. (2000). The paradox of low academic achievement but high self-esteem in African American students: an attributional account. *Educational Psychology Review, 12,* 33-63.

Verkuyten, M. & Thijs, J. (2004). Psychological disidentification with the academic domain among ethnic minority adolescents in The Netherlands. British Journal of Educational Psychology, 74, 108-125.

Vereen, L.G., Butler, S.K., Willians, F.C., Darg, J.A. & Downing, T.K.E. (2006). The use of humor when counseling African American college students. *Journal of Counseling & Development, 84,* 10-17.

Watkins, D., Cheng, C. , Mpofu, E. & Olowu, S., Singh-Snegupta, S. & Regmi, M. (2003). Gender differences in self-construal: How generalizable are Western findings? *The Journal of Social Psychology, 143,* 501-519.

Wigen, K., Holen, A. & Ellingsen, O. (2005). Predicting academic success by group behavior in PBL. *Medical Teacher, 25,* 32-37.

Winnell, F.C. & Cross, W.E. (2004). The reliability and validity of big five inventory scores with African American college students. *Journal of Multicultural Counseling and Development, 32,* 18-34.

Made in the USA
San Bernardino,
CA